Investing in Your 401k Kid

From Zero to Little Financial Genius in 5 Easy Steps

By

Bret & Tracie Shroyer

INFINITY PUBLISHING

ISBN 978-0-7414-9922-6 Paperback
ISBN 978-0-7414-9923-3 eBook
Library of Congress Control Number: 2013918343

Printed in the United States of America

Published February 2014

INFINITY PUBLISHING
1094 New DeHaven Street, Suite 100
West Conshohocken, PA 19428-2713
Toll-free (877) BUY BOOK
Local Phone (610) 941-9999
Fax (610) 941-9959
Info@buybooksontheweb.com
www.buybooksontheweb.com

Preface

In 2002, exactly one year to the day after planes crashed into the World Trade Center towers, Bret and I found ourselves at the Moscow embassy filling out paperwork to adopt our three year old daughter. As we signed the paperwork, the kind women on the other side of the desk said to us, “This is a very sad day for your country, but I hope that it will now be a very happy day in your hearts.”

From the time we decided to adopt from Russia, we knew we would probably have an uphill battle. Our process went smoothly, but we were constantly reminded of the pitfalls of Russian adoptions as news reports of severely disturbed children seemed to bombard us at every turn. We were lucky. God was watching over our family and chose the perfect little girl for us to raise and love. The details of how we know that to be true could make an entire book itself, but our daughter was healthy, happy and well adjusted. We knew as early as kindergarten, however, when her near-to-retirement teacher told us she’s never experienced learning difficulties like our daughter had, that it would be up to us to make sure she was well equipped to face the world.

For several years we plodded along. We hired tutors, enrolled her in after school enrichment programs and generally focused on her abc’s and 123’s. We figured that as long as she knew how to read, write and do math, all would be well in her world.

But then came 2007 and 2008. By late 2008, the world was in financial crisis. Bret had just lost his job as CFO of a startup, and people all around us were losing their homes to foreclosure. As we watched the news each night, it became very apparent to us that we were part of a generation of people who didn't understand the first thing about basic money management. We looked at our children and realized that if we wanted things to be different for them, it was up to us to make it so. This was most important when it came to our daughter. If ever we wanted her to be able to live on her own, to manage her own life, it was imperative that she learn how to manage money. So we shifted our thinking from math, reading and writing, to basic life skills and we started with money management. As a teenager today, she still may not be able to do long division, but she can balance a checkbook, understands interest and basic investing and knows that she never wants to be without a cushion in her savings account again (details of that story are in the book).

Our process for teaching the kids how to manage money certainly raised a lot of eyebrows. Family members thought we were nuts, the kids' friends thought we were rock stars. In the end, through lots of trial and error, we found a process that worked. We have teenagers who today know more about managing money than many adults. When others have seen how this works, they ask about it. The same friends and family members who once thought we were crazy are now asking us for details on how we got here. We realized that there are a lot more kids in the world who could benefit from the same lessons ours learned, but their parents didn't know where to start. So we wrote it all down, in a step-by-step process for others to follow. It is our belief that all kids, teenagers, even adults, must learn these basic money principles or we will be ruined as a nation.

Tracie

Contents

Why Did You Buy This Book?

Kids have been earning allowances forever. No big deal.

We both earned allowances when we were young, too. But we didn't *learn* about money until after we had made enough money to make some big mistakes. Bret was voted "most likely to succeed" by his high school classmates; it was probably expected that he had learned everything he needed to know about money in school.

The truth is this: **school isn't going to teach your kids to manage money**. The global debt-driven economic disaster that started in 2008 has shown us this statement is true. It gets worse: after elementary school math, most kids will never talk about money in school again. The best you can hope for is that schools will teach your kids to identify and count money and to make correct change. This will minimally qualify them for a job at McDonald's.

Immediately after graduation, our consumption-oriented economy gives kids the opportunity to begin building their own debt burden. They will get student loans and preapproved credit card offers; they will be offered leases on new cars with zero money down; and they will learn that they can get furniture for their apartments with "no payments for twelve months." Will they take the bait? If they're like most kids in America, nothing they have learned in school will have taught them that these are bad ideas.

There is one very important truth about money that nobody taught us in school—something we had to figure out on our own: **debt is slavery.**

You love your kids. You want them to be happy. But most of all, you want them to have the ability to move out and be independent once they're adults. When they are twenty-six, you don't want them moving back home for a few years to live in your basement—while you bail them out of their latest financial messes. This book will help you put your kids on the path to avoiding the debt trap and experiencing financial freedom.

This is going to be a lot like potty training.

What your child has to learn are very simple concepts—but it's going to get a little messy along the way. As you read this book and try to apply what we suggest, you will probably find that not everything works exactly as described on the first try. Every kid is different! As the parent, though, you know the end goal and can adjust as needed to stay on the right track.

If you keep the big picture in mind and are open to putting forth the effort suggested in this book, we promise that your kids will develop an increased financial awareness. It's going to require a little bit of creativity and flexibility on your part, as every family and every kid have unique needs.

The good news is that we have three kids—each incredibly different from the other—and these techniques are working well for all three. The process hasn't been without some fits and starts, and on occasion it has required varying degrees of handholding and modification, but it *is* working. We have confidence that all three are going to get to the finish line—financial responsibility and independence—but each will get there at his or her own pace.

With some time, effort, and creativity, you can follow this guide to get there with your kids, too.

Getting the Most from the Book

Here's what we recommend for best results:

1. Read the entire book from start to finish. Have your parenting partner do the same.
2. Go back to the beginning, reread each section, and answer the Thinking Points at the end with your partner. Some of these Thinking Points may involve homework or research on your part.
3. Start implementing! If you're really impatient, here's a peek ahead at the recommended timeline:
    - Ages four and under: start with the section called "Learning about Money."
    - Ages four to six: use the Treat Sheet to encourage saving toward a goal.
    - Ages six to nine: use a small allowance, weekly at first, to manage charity, savings, and fun, to teach the basics of budgeting.
    - Ages nine and up: work toward a larger allowance, eventually given monthly, that covers all of the child's annual expenses.
4. After a few months, go back and read through the relevant chapters again, noting what works and how you've modified the plan. This isn't a short-term process. Making these concepts stick with your kids will take time and patience—but your patience will be well rewarded!

Beginnings

The idea of money having value is not a natural concept. Preschoolers understand that a quarter is "a money" and that "a money" can buy things like treats and puppies and games. They also start with the notion that value is proportional to size: a nickel is worth more than a dime, and all paper money is a "dollar," regardless of the denomination.

One of the first big frustrations a parent faces in teaching kids about money is explaining its value. Aside from gold and silver coins, our money has no intrinsic value. There is no reason that a one-dollar bill is worth less than a hundred-dollar bill, other than the number of zeros printed on it. A preschooler can't be expected to understand why this is true—indeed, most adults would have trouble explaining why this is true. Nevertheless, it is our job as parents to impress the value of money upon youngsters—and in doing so, establish a yardstick by which he'll be able to judge the material value of everything else in his world.

Learning about Money

A child of two or three years old may not understand money but understands well the concept of "mine." That same child also understands that with a little effort, he can make something that is "not mine" into something that is "mine." At the earliest ages, this means simply taking it from the rightful owner. Only later will he understand that it takes money to get the things that he wants. What he will really learn is this: **money is the way we store value earned through work.**

Let's investigate that idea more fully.

When someone performs work, he does so only with the agreement that his labor will be rewarded with something of value.

You can work for a farmer and harvest fifty bushels of apples in exchange for one bushel of those apples. But what if you don't want apples? What if you want a pair of socks instead?

In a money-free world, you could trade with the woman who knits socks. Now she has performed work (knitting socks) in exchange for apples, and you've harvested apples in exchange for socks.

As the economy gets bigger, you can see how using money helps make this process easier. Add in a butcher, a carpenter, and a doctor, and you have a lot of work ahead of you organizing all the apple trading to get what you need. With the introduction of money, everyone in society can value his work in terms of one common unit (such as the dollar) rather than thinking about what the work is worth in terms of apples, socks, bacon, or surgeries.

Money is also beneficial in that it acts to store the value of work. Now suppose you want to buy a cow instead of socks. How many bushels of apples would you have to earn before you could trade them for a cow? You would obviously have to save up a lot of apples. Could you keep all of those apples from spoiling? Here is where money shines: if the apple farmer pays you in coin for your work, you can save some of those coins—for years, if needed—until you have enough to buy your cow.

There is a flip side to this, however. If money is the store of value already earned through work, then debt is the promise to repay value through future work. **Taking on debt today is the same thing as making an agreement to work without payment tomorrow.** What do you call someone who is forced to work without pay?

It is worth repeating: **debt is slavery.**

When our youngest son was nine, he gave his grandpa a certificate for Father's Day that said, "Good for eight hours of yard work." This wasn't a huge commitment; after all, how much work can you really get out of a nine-year-old? Well, Grandpa saved that certificate and then cashed it in five years later—and our son spent a July day digging trenches by hand to install a new irrigation system. Normally, Grandpa pays well for help around the yard and probably would have paid at least fifty dollars for the trench digging. It was hard work! But since our son had given the coupon as a gift, he was "in debt" to Grandpa, obligated to work that debt off for free. You can bet that future coupons will come with expiration dates!

If the goal is to stay out of debt, then what's the strategy to achieve that goal? We started by teaching our kids how to save.

Thinking Points

- How do you, as a parent, teach the value of money?
- What do you remember about learning the value of money?
- When did you learn how to make change?
- How often do your children see coins and paper money?
- Are you modeling the act of saving up for later?
- What treats or toys does your child have trouble saving up for later?

Saving for Later

So, we've taught our children about money; now we have to teach them what it means to save. Money as stored value has no meaning if they don't understand the basic idea of saving something for later. What's the first step in getting a child to understand the concept of saving?

[1]

Baby Step Zero: teach the concept of saving by using Goldfish snack crackers.

Do this: on Monday, hand your child a small jar (recycle a peanut butter jar or a baby food jar) with twenty-eight Goldfish crackers in it. Have another jar with the same amount of crackers in it for yourself. Proudly announce, "This week, we're going to have a special snack every day before dinner! While we're getting ready for dinner, we can have four Goldfish appetizers. Doesn't that sound like fun?"

Have your child keep the Goldfish jar on the counter in the kitchen next to your jar and let him know that those are his crackers

[1] Image © by Evan-Amos http://commons.wikimedia.org/wiki/File:Goldfish-Crackers.jpg

that he can eat whenever he likes. You, however, will consistently eat four Goldfish before every meal. Make a scene of it! Say, "It's almost dinner time! I can't wait to have my Goldfish appetizers!" And then go to your jar and dole out your four Goldfish.

You can expect that Junior will have some fits and starts in the beginning; he'll eat some Goldfish during the day, or he'll want to eat more than four at a meal. By dinnertime on Sunday, you will still have four Goldfish, but he will have none.

A two- or three-year-old child hates this. In his world, it is absolutely not fair that you have Goldfish and he doesn't. Hold firm, don't give in, and **don't preach**! Instead, be sympathetic[2]: "Oh dear! I'm sorry you're out of Goldfish. I'm really enjoying my Goldfish appetizers. I can understand why you might feel bad that you don't have any, because I know how much you love Goldfish, too." Feel free to go over the top, and really enjoy your Goldfish. The pain will help Junior learn to save Goldfish over the course of the week, so he will have the same amount as you every day.

For an extra level of reinforcement, you can introduce the idea of "buying" something with the Goldfish. For example, what would happen if someone else in the house had some Oreo cookies and was willing to "sell" them for three Goldfish each? Be creative—start with Goldfish and then find ways to get your child to exchange them for something bigger during appetizer time.

You can expect this to take some time to master—don't give up. Let him learn and understand what it means to save something for later. The key to success, as with most anything in life, is to be consistent. If you do this activity for only one week, you may not see results. If you forget to talk about it before dinner each night, the value of saving is lost—he can't save Goldfish if he isn't thinking

---

[2] This approach to parenting, by the way, is one of the core principles of the Love and Logic Institute, an organization "dedicated to making parenting and teaching fun and rewarding, instead of stressful and chaotic." Love and Logic philosophy advises that children learn best when they're given a task and allowed to make their own choices and experience failure when the cost of failure is still small. These failures are met with love and empathy by the parents and teachers. For more information on this wonderful program, see http://LoveAndLogic.com

about Goldfish at all. Finally, if your family eats Goldfish on a regular basis, you would be better off choosing a different treat.

In the late 1960s, psychologist Walter Mischel led a series of experiments now known as the Stanford marshmallow experiment. In these studies, kids were offered a choice: receive one marshmallow now, or wait fifteen minutes and receive two marshmallows.

Ten years later, Mischel did a follow-up study and discovered that the kids who had chosen to wait for two marshmallows were more likely to place higher on competency tests as teenagers. Another follow-up study showed that these teens also achieved higher SAT exam scores.

You may already have a financial Einstein in the family, and the first time you try this experiment, Junior might surprise you by saving all of the Goldfish, just as you asked. This is a win! You don't have to teach the importance of saving; he already understands.

Thinking Points

- Is your child generally impatient?
- Do your kids already understand the idea of “saving for later” with something other than money? How can you leverage this into learning about saving money?
- Is there a favorite small snack that might work better than Goldfish? Maybe stickers? Make sure you stock up before you get started.
- What is your initial allotment of “treats” going to be? How does that break down per day?
- When will you introduce this plan to your kids? What materials (snacks, jars, sheets) do you need to gather first?
- How will you react as a parent if your child has a tantrum after not saving enough Goldfish to eat? What will be your response? What will be your strategy for making this a teaching moment?

Beyond Goldfish

Once you have cleared this hurdle and have taught what it means to save, you'll find yourself in the following situation: you reach the checkout lane at the store with your child, and he sees his favorite candy or gum.

He reaches for it and declares, "Mine!" At that point, you are at a crossroads: have an argument right there in the checkout lane or give in and buy the pack of gum to restore the peace. (Of course, there's a third option—after you tell him no, he looks back at you and says, "Okay, Mommy." But that wouldn't make a very good illustration, now would it?)

In general, we advocate that you shouldn't buy your child a treat just to avoid an argument or tantrum. But there's nothing wrong with buying your child a treat every now and again, particularly if he's being a joy. In that case it's a really good idea to emphasize, "You are being so polite and respectful! You've made me so happy, I feel like buying you a little treat."

Making a habit of giving in to avoid drama is not an ideal solution and will probably lead to more drama the next time you're in the store. Instead, try this: before you go to the store, give your child four quarters and tell him that he will be able to use them to buy a special treat at the checkout lane.

Remember, a treat is a *treat*. Although you'll certainly need to put some parameters on what he's buying, try not to be too restrictive. Help him pick out a one-dollar item, then take the treat to the cashier to complete the transaction. In this way, you're reinforcing the concept that money can be exchanged for treats and that even a child can buy treats.

Thinking Points

- How much money are you comfortable giving your kids to spend in the store on a treat? Make sure you have that amount in change.

Baby Step One: give your child money before you enter the store, and help him buy a treat when you get to the checkout.

When kids first have money and freedom, it's a lot of fun to see what they choose and how they put together the pieces of learning to make a purchase.

It is important that you don't wait until you're at the checkout to give your child the money. Let him have it when you enter the store (or even at home) to discourage begging in the checkout aisle.

After several trips to the store using this strategy, what happens is this: instead of asking for treats at the store, your child will start asking you for money instead. You win! Give him the dollar and mentally prepare to move on to the next step—earning and saving quarters at home.

Above all, be flexible!

Will it be a problem for you to let your child pick out a treat while you're shopping? If your child has allergies, for example, or you don't allow sugar at home, make sure to find an area of the store where you can allow him to shop without restriction. Maybe it's not at the grocery store, but another store that sells fun, inexpensive items. Other examples include choosing a dessert next time the family goes out for dinner or picking out a small treat for the dog at the pet store.

Whatever you do, keep it fun! If you put too many restrictions on the activity, your child will sense that you're not happy about the exercise, and the learning opportunity will be lost. Remember, your goal here isn't to create a little shopping monster but rather to find something he already enjoys in life and to show him how he can get it at a store in exchange for money.

Baby Step Two: give your child money at home—with a catch!

Once you are both comfortable with the idea of using money to buy small items at the store, you are ready for the next phase. The next time you're getting ready to hand out quarters, tell your child, "Oh dear! I'm almost out of quarters. I only have one left, but I have an idea of how we can save quarters to buy a treat the next time we go to the store. Would you like to hear my idea?" Hopefully you can sell this in an exciting, attractive way to help your child start saving money. Instead of a teaching moment, this is now a project—an adventure that you and your child will engage in together.

Take out a large piece of paper and show your child how to trace four circles on the paper using the quarter as a template. Then help him to tape the first quarter onto one of the circles and explain that as he collects quarters, he can tape those onto the paper as well. When he has four quarters, he'll have enough to buy a treat the next time you go to the store. To help him remember why he's collecting quarters, you can also tape a picture of his favorite treat or an empty treat wrapper on the paper. This visual reminder further reinforces the goal of saving all four quarters.

After doing this a few times, you can use a ready-made page like the one pictured. Highlight the quarters that need to be filled in and have your child put a picture or drawing of what he is saving for in the "My Goal" box.

Treat Sheet

Money Needed:

My Goal:

Instructions: Place a photo or drawing in the "Goal" box
Highlight the money needed to buy the goal
Help your child fill in the required money with tape
When the goal is completely filled in, go shopping!

For older kids, this exercise might involve dollar bills instead of quarters. You can save dollar bills, for example, to buy a four-dollar box of cereal (the sugary kind Mom usually won't buy). Not only will this reinforce the idea of saving paper money, it will also help your child understand that TV-advertised sugar cereal is really expensive stuff. It does not work well to tape dollar bills onto a page like this (they're bigger than you think!). You can put check boxes on the page to represent dollars saved or use a jar with a Post-it note on top to keep track of progress toward the goal.

We call the savings plan page our "Treat Sheet." You can find a copy on the Resources page at http://401kKid.com/downloads.

You can use items other than "treats" for the savings goal. When our kids were in elementary school, one of our nonfood favorites was the Scholastic Book Club book orders that the kids brought home from school. Honestly, we didn't need any more books in the house, but there's nothing quite as satisfying to a kid as getting a new book on book order day in kindergarten.

We helped our kids to save their dollars and pick out books on the order form. Much happiness ensued! They took extra pride in telling their teachers, “I paid for this book all by myself!” As an added bonus, they seemed to enjoy reading “their” books more than the books we bought for them.

Now that there is a goal in mind on the Treat Sheet, how is he going to get the rest of those quarters?

Thinking Points

Set up your scenario:

- When is your next planned trip to the store? Do you need to plan one that doesn’t coincide with your own personal shopping in case there is a tantrum or things don’t go as planned?
- Where will you shop? Which areas of that store are good for your child to choose his treat?
- When will you talk to your child about what’s going to happen?

Quarters for Jobs

One easy way to get money into your kids' hands is through specific jobs. This mechanism is separate from a periodic allowance (covered in another section) and is simply an agreement between you and your child: "If you'd like to help me with some of my chores, I'd be happy to pay you. This job pays a quarter." Make a deliberate distinction that this is a "job" you'd like his help in doing.

At age two or three, a child will have very few chores, maybe none that are performed solo. Some **chores** might be:

- Making his bed in the morning
- Putting his dirty clothes in the laundry basket
- Putting away his toys when he's done playing
- Carrying his plate to the sink after dinner

At this age, the main idea of chores is: "I'm learning how to clean up after myself." We don't reward these tasks with treats or money—they are the child's contribution to the family.

So what kinds of **jobs** might be appropriate for a child of two or three years old?

- Helping to sweep the kitchen floor (or at least making an honest attempt to move the dirt around)
- Helping to put away the groceries
- Picking up the dog's toys
- Filling the dog's food or water dish
- Cleaning with a hand-held vacuum cleaner

Chores vs. Jobs

Chores are the things we expect each member of the family to do on a regular basis without any reward. They are your baseline contribution to the family.

Jobs are something over and above your regular chores; therefore, you can earn a reward (a quarter) for completing a job.

The difference is not just semantic—as a parent, you perform **chores** every day without any fanfare or reward, but when you perform at your **job**, you get paid.

- Arranging the shoes at the back door

These jobs, distinct from chores, are tasks the child is taking on to help someone else or to clean up after someone else. Again, chores are a minimal contribution to the family; jobs are over and above the expected chores.

Many of these jobs will be performed with direct supervision, and you may need to redo them later (for example, sweeping) because a young child can't be expected to do the job thoroughly. Nevertheless, it's a good idea to give your child plenty of opportunities to do these extra jobs. Not only will they earn rewards, they will learn discipline and feel the satisfaction that comes from a job well done. It is also important to make sure that you are giving them kudos for the jobs they attempt to do and that the jobs match their ability level. You want them to view their jobs as pleasant and positive experiences.

Thinking Points

- What are some jobs that your child can accomplish independently?
- Can your child come up with ideas for new paying jobs? What will she come up with if you ask her to suggest jobs?
- Are paying jobs always available, or do regular chores have to be finished first?

Visual Goals: Setting Your Sights Higher

A child of two or three years is a very literal, concrete thinker. A Treat Sheet—a single piece of paper with outlines for four quarters and a wrapper from a roll of Life Savers—is a very visual, concrete tool he can use to save toward a goal.

You will probably find that it's very easy for your child to do enough jobs to save four quarters—and you might start feeling pressure from him to take more frequent outings to the store. Make an effort at first to go to the store more often. It will be worth it. Within a very short time, your child will realize that special treasures from the store don't come from whining, begging, or tantrums, but from money that must first be earned through work at home.

The next step in expanding this idea is to find a larger goal—a small toy, a game, or a movie, for example. When your child identifies such an item at the store as something he wants, say this: "Wow! That looks awesome! I bet you'd really love to have that, wouldn't you? Well, it's five whole dollars. How about when we get home, we make up a Treat Sheet to save quarters to buy it?"

Make it exciting and follow up when you get home by creating the Treat Sheet. If the desired treat is five dollars or more, your child will probably be surprised at how many circles he has to draw on the sheet! It's a great visual cue, however, that explains the relative value of the new treat—a game is much more valuable than a small bag of M&M'S. Remember to put a visual cue to the new treat on the page, as well. Have your child draw a picture of the new goal or find a picture in a store ad and paste that on the sheet.

Thinking Points

- Will it work to have your child save up the full amount for these larger treats, or do you want him to save up only a portion of the purchase price?
- In the beginning, goals should be able to be achieved in a week or so. What are some small goals you could start out with?
- As the child learns how to save, the time frame for achieving the goal can be extended, but having a goal that's too big can be counter-productive. What's your child's current attention span when it comes to saving toward a goal?

Always Have a Goal

The treat sheet helps solve another parenting problem—it's a focal point for the bored or misdirected child. We've found great value in using the Treat Sheet and in always having a current goal in progress. This way, if you ever hear, "I'm bored!" you can respond, "Well, have you earned all of the money toward your goal yet?" As they get older, you will probably find that you'll need larger and larger goals to keep them occupied.

Baby Step Three: continue making goals larger and larger.

Your biggest problem might be maintaining a large enough list of jobs that you can refer to when your child is looking for a paying job. We've found that it works well to **ask the child to suggest a job**—you will be surprised what he identifies as needing to be done around the house. Our back closet has been the frequent victim of thorough cleanings over the years as a result of the kids being a few dollars short of their goals.

One year, we created a stretch goal for our kids. We told them that Mom would be going to visit Grandma and Grandpa in Arizona over spring break. Dad would be staying home for work. Anyone who wanted to go with Mom was welcome to do so. However, plane tickets were very expensive, and we didn't have the money to pay for three extra tickets.

To help them visualize their progress toward the goal of a $160 plane ticket, we created a poster-sized Treat Sheet. This allowed them to see that, over many months, they were getting closer and closer to the goal. It encouraged them to keep doing jobs and saving their earnings for the trip.

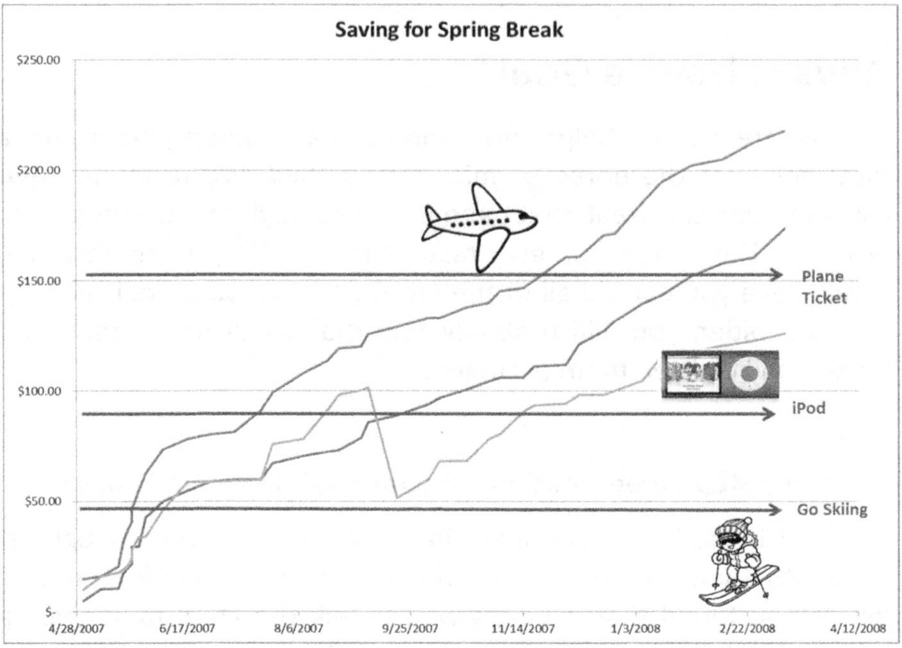

This chart provided a lot of insight into the way our kids think. One was seven and two were eight years old at the time. To show them how expensive a plane ticket was, we included other items on the chart that they were more familiar with—a photo from an ad for an iPod, and a picture from a local ski resort. We put all of those items on one side of the chart along with the dollar amount to match. We then drew lines for each kid that showed how much money they had saved in relation to each of those items. We found that the boys kept their focus on the plane ticket and willingly passed up the other items in favor of watching their line grow.

On the other hand, when our daughter saw her line "hit" those other items, she immediately wanted to go to Target to purchase whatever it was. After explaining to her a few times that if she kept spending what she had saved, she would never be able to afford a plane ticket, we decided to let her learn the lesson for herself. That's right—when it came time to buy the tickets, she didn't get one. She had chosen to buy an iPod Shuffle instead and didn't have enough money left to buy the plane ticket.

Since Bret was staying home to work, she stayed with him. We can't say that she wasn't bummed when everyone else got dropped off at the airport, but the two of them had a good time while Tracie and the boys enjoyed sunny Phoenix. After all, she wasn't being punished; she had just made different choices about how to spend her money. This one experience when she was eight years old made a big impact. Now as a teenager, she consistently has more money in her savings account than either of her brothers.

When we tell this story, people are amazed that we didn't bail her out. In fact, a television reporter interviewing our family heard our daughter tell this story and literally had to stop the interview to regroup because he was sure that he'd heard it wrong.

Were we tempted to bail her out? Of course! It's hard for any parent to see one of their kids in a tough spot. After discussing it, we decided that giving her the money to buy the ticket would send a terrible message not only to her but also to our two sons who had worked hard to save for the trip.

The boys were so proud to tell Grandma and Grandpa of their success, and our daughter still talks about how she learned the importance of saving from this event.

Baby Step Four: understanding the value of money.

This isn't really a "step" but an end point. When your child can select and understand a goal that will require two or more months of work and saving, you can be confident that he understands enough about the value of money to move on to a larger financial task like managing a monthly allowance.

Thinking Points

- What are some big goals you can get your child to start thinking about right now?

Starting an Allowance

When your child has a thorough understanding of the value of money—at least in his limited world of treats, games, and toys—it's time to introduce an allowance.

What's an Allowance?

The topic of allowance has gotten a lot of press lately, and a lot of the conversation has been about what to call it: allowance, salary, contribution, shares. Our opinion is that there is too much focus on what it's called—a detail that doesn't really matter in the end. For the rest of the book, we will call it an allowance, primarily because that's what we have always called it in our family. If you prefer a different name, go ahead and use it.

Here's the dirty little secret: **an allowance is not a handout but a new delegation of responsibility from the parent to the child.**

> ***When can we start an allowance?***
>
> Every child is going to be different. Our youngest child went to a partial allowance (just a couple of categories) at age seven and a full allowance at age nine. With some help and training, most kids should be ready for the full allowance between the ages of ten and thirteen.

We are pretty explicit with our kids—everything in the family is communal property, and the parents are responsible for making sure everyone and everything is properly cared for. If kids show responsibility, we'll delegate some of our responsibility to them. If they are not, then we reserve the right to start making the decisions again. It is important to note that regardless of how poor they are at making responsible choices, we will still use the family's resources to provide them with clothing, shoes, food, and health care—it's our job as parents to make sure they have whatever they truly need. (And if resources are limited, it's also our job to distinguish "needs" from "wants.")

When you give your child an allowance, you're not simply giving him money; you're giving him freedom to decide how to spend the family's money. Best of all, starting an allowance won't cost you a dime because his allowance will just be some of the money that you were going to spend on his behalf anyway.

What's the right age to start an allowance? It depends on when you are able to get your child to advance to Baby Step Four: Understanding the value of money." Once he understands the value of money and can save several months toward a goal, he's ready for an allowance.

To explain a successful allowance system, it makes sense to start at the end at the teenage level to see how all of the pieces fit together. You can then scale back to something appropriate for the age of your child.

How much money do you spend on your kids?

Every year new research emerges with the sole intent of making us gasp in shock at how much we will spend on our children before they turn eighteen. The figures are shocking because, frankly, not many parents carefully track how much money they actually spend on their kids.

If you don't already track your expenses, you might wish to start not only to facilitate the allowance process but for your own financial health. And remember, starting an allowance won't cost you anything; you're using money that you would have spent on your kids anyway and giving them the responsibility to decide how to spend it.

A good starting point is to evaluate your spending over the last year. If you don't keep detailed records, then you may not know exactly what you spent on clothing, shoes, activities, and food (among other categories). Don't worry! Start with a good estimate. If you later discover that your estimate was too low, you can increase the allowance or choose to pay for some larger items (which is what you're already doing). This is a multi-year process; after two years you'll have everything pretty well dialed in.

Once you have a good estimate of how much money you're spending on your kids, divide it into categories. At ages ten and eleven, our kids were each costing us about $125 per month, or $1,500 per year. We're not talking about "spending money" here—we're talking about all of the money we spend on them in a year in the following categories:

- Clothing
- Shoes
- Food
- Activities
- Fun

Now that they are older, they're starting to push that budget up; clothing is more expensive, activities cost more, and they are simply more involved, so we have increased their monthly allowances to $160. Remember, the allowance isn't a "gift." It's money that we must spend on our kids because they are our dependents. You may spend considerably more or less on your kids depending on your resources, your kids' ages, and what sorts of activities they're involved in.

> ***Choices!***
>
> Kids love choosing how they spend their money. We wanted to reinforce the fun side of saving—what good is saving money if you can't spend it? We helped each child set a savings goal: Two chose to save $160 toward a plane ticket to see Grandma. The third chose to save eighty-five dollars to buy an iPod. They all met their goals!

When you first start an allowance, you will probably choose just one category, such as food, which will let your child practice making his own choices. For example, he can use his allowance to buy school lunch, desserts at school, treats at the store, or candy at the movies.

Thinking Points

- How much are you spending every month (or every year) on your kids?
- Will you feel a sense of relief not having to make all of the decisions for your child?
- How will your relationship with your child change when he or she is no longer giving you a shopping list or expressing unhappiness with your buying decisions?

Budgeting for Kids

Once we had the $1,500 per year target established, we sat down with each kid and had a talk about his or her monthly allowance. The primary purpose of this meeting was to let the kids know that they would be receiving significant allowances every month and **that they would be trusted with deciding how to spend them.** This was a very interesting moment, like the scene in *Austin Powers: International Man of Mystery* where Dr. Evil puts his pinky to his mouth and says, "One million dollars!"

We were clear that their allowances were our money, not their money—if they could not demonstrate responsibility in managing and spending this money, we would take the allowances back and spend the money for them, just as we had been doing their whole lives.

The second big task of this meeting was to allocate their monthly allowance ($125) into various spending categories. Our children's budgets looked like this:

> ***Golden shoes?***
>
> While shoe shopping with our ten-year-old son, we were distracted by a similarly aged kid and his mother who were shopping nearby. The mother and son were deadlocked in an argument over a sixty-dollar pair of Nikes. Without thinking about it, our son blurted out, "I wouldn't pay sixty dollars for shoes if they were made of gold!" The mother and son quickly left—without the shoes.

Monthly Allowance

	Son	Daughter
Clothing	$15	$30
Shoes	$15	$25
Food	$10	$5
Activities	$50	$30
Fun	$5	$5
Presents	$10	$10
Charity	$10	$10
Savings	$10	$10
Total	**$125**	**$125**

Let's talk about a few significant items regarding budgeting:

- Your child is unqualified to engage in a budgeting discussion if he does not have an **understanding of the value of money** and an appreciation for the cost of the goods and services in his life. Only when you've finished the baby steps in the previous sections can you be sure he's ready for this responsibility.
- Because he understands the value of money, he will be **completely blown away at the size of his monthly budget**. If a child is used to managing money in five- and ten-dollar increments, having a fresh $125 at the start of each month will be overwhelming. Don't worry, you will be working with him for at least the first year.
- You will be surprised at how the **dollars stretch much further** when he is managing the spending. It's easy to "need" a new pair of cool shoes when your parents are buying them for you. But when he saves three months to buy a pair of shoes, that same seventy-five dollars can buy three (or more!) pairs on sale at a discount department store.
- Instead of dread, you will feel a sense of liberation taking your children shopping. You don't have to make choices or find good bargains—you've handed off that responsibility to the children. Additionally, it's always more fun to help others spend their money while you don't have to spend a dime. (Well, technically it's still your money; it just feels like theirs.)
- When your kids make their own buying decisions, **there's not much for them to argue about with you**. Hello, family happiness!
- Did you notice the three new categories? The presents category is a place to accumulate funds to buy birthday and Christmas presents for friends and family. Charity and savings are cornerstones of successful money management and will be discussed later.

Our kids were quite young when we started this system. Because we had been tracking our budget items for years on

Quicken, we had a good idea of how much money should go into each category. We set up the budget accordingly. If you have older kids, have them help you set up how much money will go into each category and then re-evaluate after a few months. In our opinion, it is beneficial to take advantage of every opportunity to have a conversation about money with your kids.

Thinking Points

- What shopping disagreements have you had with your kids? How might those change using this new system?
- If your child chooses to spend half of her clothing budget on one pair of jeans instead of buying several pairs on sale, what consequences will she face? Can she live with those consequences? Can you?
- Just because your child is carefully managing a clothing budget doesn't mean that all of her clothes are going to come from that budget. Parents and grandparents love to be generous and especially love it when kids appreciate their generosity. Suddenly, clothes as Christmas presents are going to seem a lot more precious. Don't be afraid to make a spontaneous gift of a needed article every now and again—the fact that you made the effort and went above and beyond the budget will be very appreciated.

Budgeting in Action

Now it's time to act on everything we've learned so far.

Step One: buy a coupon organizer.

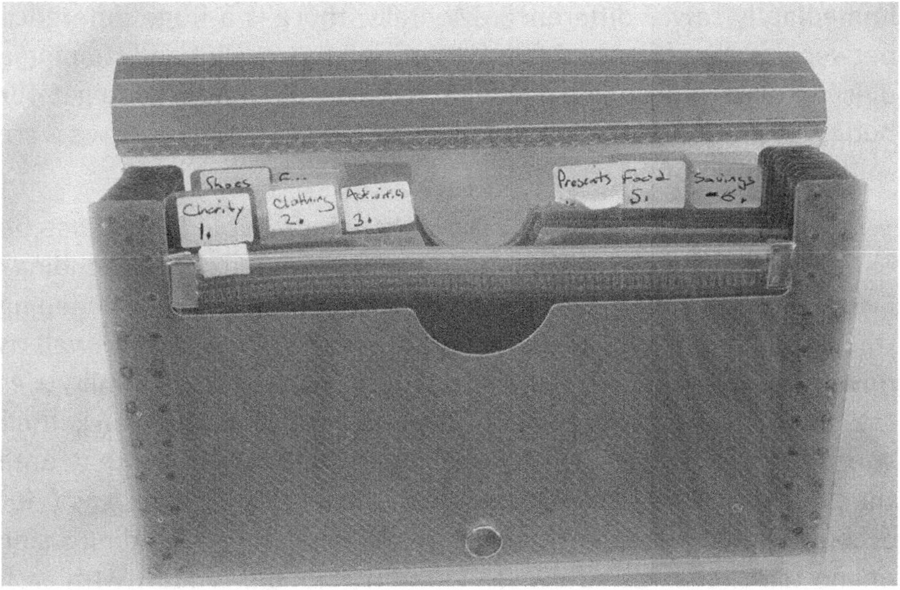

We've tried a lot of different methods, and by far the easiest solution to managing a budget is with a coupon organizer. It can be utilitarian (as in the picture) or it can look a lot like a wallet—either way, it will do a great job organizing the money in individual spending categories.

There is a significant benefit in having tangible paper money in each of the category folders rather than one lump sum of money or—even worse—a prepaid debit card that is refreshed every month. Until kids are proficient at staying within a budget, by category, month after month, we strongly recommend segregated sums of physical cash in each category. Debit cards have their place but not until much later.

A word about the difference cash can make: A few years ago, we went through Dave Ramsey's Financial Peace University. Although we had been budgeting our own spending for years, we both used debit cards to make things "easier." Even though we did a good job of staying within our budget, we were always just a little bit short at the end of each month. We decided to set aside the debit cards and use Ramsey's recommended cash system, and we immediately saw a difference. Mentally, there is a huge difference between pulling twenty-dollar bills out of your wallet and running a piece of plastic through a machine. Not only did it help us to get our budget in line, it also helped our kids to see when and how we were spending our money.

What about electronic record keeping? Wouldn't it just be easier to have the kids use an online tool to keep track of spending? Eventually, yes. There are some great tools out there for keeping track of spending that are easy enough for kids to use as well as powerful enough to satisfy the needs of parents. Our family uses the free online service Goodbudget to help the kids track their spending and budgets. However, experience taught us that until the kids could manage their money using cold hard cash for accounting, they weren't ready to manage their spending using online tools. Even as adults we found it valuable to start with cash and a physical register when we were learning how to manage our finances. The hands-on record keeping was something that we could feel and understand. When we moved to electronic record keeping later, we were able to maintain the discipline we'd developed using pen and paper.

Step Two: meet monthly.

Consistency is important. Our family has monthly allowance meetings on the first Friday of the month. This works well for us because we both get paid on the first of the month; so the first Friday is always on or after payday. It is also helpful to have a consistent allowance day and for it to occur weekly. Kids' lives operate on more of a weekly rather than a monthly cycle. The allowance meetings aren't the same as family meetings. (We hold family meetings twice each year: once when school starts and again when school ends for the summer. We have the kids lay out everyone's responsibilities and chores for the coming season. You can find a sample agenda and more about family meetings on our Resources page at http://401kkid.com/downloads.)

Bret meets one-on-one with each kid to go over his or her monthly expenses. Very important discussions about money, budgeting, and even basic math have occurred during these meetings, so doing them individually has proven to be most effective. You can see a checklist and a video example of one our monthly budget meetings at http://401kkid.com/downloads.

Tracie doesn't participate in these meetings; Bret found that the kids were a lot more open with their money issues when Mom wasn't around, especially if one of them had "lost" some money in a month, resulting in a stressful meeting. You will have to see what kind of meeting arrangement works for your family!

Step Three: reconcile the previous month's expenses.

This is important! If there's something fundamentally wrong with the way your child is managing his allowance, you want to know right away, not after five months (and $500) has been wasted.

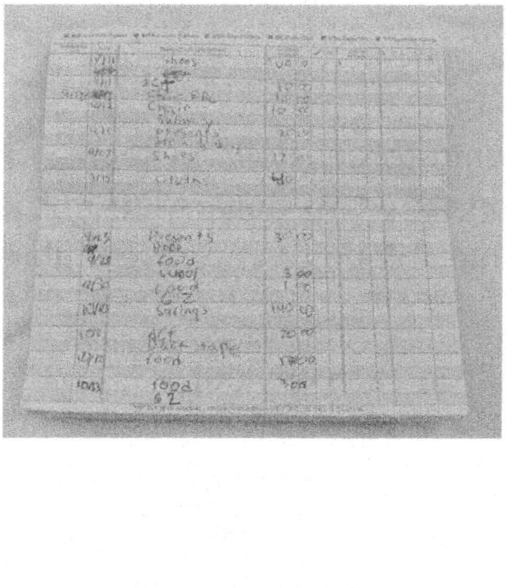

Our kids use a checkbook register and, yes, they learned to do this at age nine. It's good practice to use a register, it fits nicely into the coupon organizer, and learning to balance a checkbook is not a skill they're going to learn in most schools. Even if you don't use a check register to track your finances, you should be using *something*, and your kids should get in the habit of tracking their spending, as well.

Every time your child takes money out of a category (or puts money in), he places an entry in the register. On allowance day, he adds up all of the monthly changes in the register by category. Bret then enters that into the reconciliation spreadsheet on Google Docs. (You can find this spreadsheet and more resources at http://401kkid.com/downloads.)

The final step is to count the remaining money in each envelope. If all categories balance, then the child has correctly managed all of his money that month.

This is an excerpt from the monthly reconciliation worksheet. It shows that the child started the month with eighty-five dollars in his clothing budget and twenty-five dollars in shoes.

	Clothing	Shoes
Starting Balance	$85	$25

He then goes to his checkbook register that he uses to track spending and adds up all of the money spent on clothing and shoes. This month he spent twenty-three dollars on clothing and nothing on shoes.

	Clothing	Shoes
Starting Balance	$85	$25
Monthly Expense	$23	$0
Expected Balance	**$62 ($85-$23)**	**$25 ($25-$0)**

Since the register indicates twenty-three dollars spent on clothing for the month, there should be sixty-two dollars left in the clothing envelope. Similarly, there should still be twenty-five dollars in the shoes envelope.

Now he counts how much is actually in each envelope.

	Clothing	Shoes
Starting Balance	$85	$25
Monthly Expense	$23	$0
Expected Balance	$62 ($85-$23)	$25 ($25-$0)
Actual Balance	**$60 (counted by kid)**	**$25 (counted by kid)**

Oops! The actual balance in the clothing envelope is only sixty dollars. This fund is out of balance by two dollars. The shoe category looks good—we expected to find twenty-five dollars and it's all still there. The discrepancy isn't an indication of a huge problem; somewhere during the month two dollars went missing. If fifty dollars went missing, we might have a heart-to-heart conversation. If it happens month after month, we might take control of the allowance until the kid can start exhibiting more response-bility. In our family, if every line item in the monthly statement balances on allowance day, the child earns a five-dollar bonus payment directly into the "fun" bucket. This is a huge incentive for the kids to be careful when tracking their spending.

> ***Responsibility***
>
> One of your key objectives during this phase is to let your children have responsibility for their own finances. Expect them to slip from time to time. The good news is, at this stage their mistakes are going to be relatively small—ten or twenty dollars—but will seem significant to them. They will remember and learn from their errors.
>
> Don't micromanage—they must make mistakes to learn the pain of financial inattention. If they're just learning this lesson at age eighteen, the mistakes will be much costlier.

Since this balance was off by two dollars, we chalk it up to a clerical error, accept the new balance, and move on. Sadly, there will be no five-dollar bonus for perfect record keeping this month.

Now he adds the new month's allowance to the envelope, and calculates the new balance:

	Clothing	Shoes
Starting Balance	$85	$25
Monthly Expense	$23	$0
Expected Balance	$62 ($85-$23)	$25 ($25-$0)
Actual Balance	$60 (counted by kid)	$25 (counted by kid)
Current Allowance	$10	$20
New Balance	**70 (60+10)**	**45 (25+20)**

We have gotten to the point where it takes just five or ten minutes for our kids to tally their monthly expenses and for Bret to enter them into the worksheet, see if they're in balance, and hand out the next month's allowance. You can get a copy of the full worksheet we use in our family, in Microsoft Excel or Google Docs format, from our Resources page.

Step Four: talk about the current month's budget.

Now that you both know how much was spent last month and how much remains in each category, you may decide to re-allocate the allowance this month. At the end of last month, sixty dollars remained in the clothing envelope. He has no plans to buy clothes this month, but he does want to buy a forty-dollar pair of boots. To accomplish this goal, we agree to decrease the clothing allowance from fifteen dollars down to ten and to move the extra five dollars into the shoes envelope.

Step Five: pay out the allowance.

Having settled on the new allocation, pay out the cash and allow your child to put it into the respective envelopes. You might consider declaring the "fun" money to be off the balance sheet—we have our kids put fun money right into their wallets with no need to reconcile. For them, fun money is considered spent as soon as they earn it. This isn't too far from the reality of the fun money we put into our own wallets.

For the next month, he is responsible for managing his money. He must note all of his expenses in the register to make sure that everything balances at the end of the month. When allowance day comes again, he has come full-circle and is further along the path to financial responsibility.

Thinking Points

- How important will you make monthly reconciliation? Will you ask for reconciliation to the penny? To the dollar? To the nearest five dollars?
- Will you give a bonus if everything reconciles?
- Will you let your child have control of the money envelope at home, or will it go in a "safe spot" under your control?

Budget Categories

One of the keys to making the budget work is reinforcing the idea that there isn't one big pile of money every month but a bunch of small piles. A second important idea to emphasize is that it is not necessary (in fact, it's discouraged!) to spend all of the money every month.

Getting a monthly budget of twenty dollars for shoes means that over the course of the year you can spend $240 on footwear. That might be fifty dollars for winter boots, three pairs of tennis shoes at thirty dollars each, dress shoes for forty dollars, three pairs of flip-flops—you get the picture. Obviously, you can't spend twenty dollars each month—you'll need to save up for several months to have funds to buy the boots.

> ***The sandwich marathon***
>
> When school lunch is free (because Mom and Dad are paying for it), most kids will opt for school lunch. A lot of parents don't like spending money on dodgy school lunches and expensive à la carte items, but let's face it: it's a hassle to pack a lunch every day.
>
> Our kids have developed a great habit of packing their own lunches each day because they know it saves them money. We make it easy on them by providing lots of lunch items such as fruit, granola bars, hard-boiled eggs, and cheese sticks. Often there are homemade sweets to include. Most importantly, we make the main course easy by hosting a bi-monthly **sandwich marathon**.
>
> We buy bread, bagels, and tortillas, along with meats, cheeses, and PB&J fixings. Tracie will even search out fun mayos, mustards, and other sandwich spreads (dill pickle relish is a favorite!). We lay it all out on the kitchen counter and the kids go to town making sandwiches. The adults wrap each one in wax paper, label it with the kid's name, and put it into a two-gallon freezer bag. For the next two months, making lunch is as easy as grabbing a sandwich from the freezer!

Similarly, the activities fund will be very cyclical. Registration for football is $110 and takes place every year in July. The Boy Scouts re-charter in January, and dues are fifty dollars. You'll probably need to help your child look ahead to upcoming months to make sure he's saving for those big purchases.

But this is going to be so expensive!

Remember: the allowance isn't "extra" money that you're giving to your kids; it's money that you would be spending on them anyway because you're a caring parent. By giving them control over the spending, you gain an additional advantage from every dollar, as you'll see next.

> ***Putting big purchases in perspective***
>
> We like our kids to go to camp for a week every summer. Not only is it a good experience for them but it gives Mom and Dad a little bit of vacation time as well. We want the kids to be invested in the camp experience, so we encourage them to help pay for it. We offer to pay for half and suggest that they fund the rest from their activities accounts (about $150).
>
> Our ten-year-old daughter balked at this—she understood that $150 was a lot of money. In the end, she agreed and went to camp.
>
> When we picked her up at the end of the week, the first thing she said was, "Camp was super fun! That was totally worth $150!"

Food

The food category covers anything edible. At our house, food in the refrigerator, freezer, or pantry is "free." Our budget covers the family groceries and dinners out; their budgets cover extras like snacks, treats, frozen yogurt, food court meals at the mall, popcorn at the movie theater, and so on. A big item for the food budget is school lunch. Our kids get lunch for free if they take a brown bag from home. They also have the option of buying lunch at school using their own funds. One kid eats fairly regularly at school and has chosen to allocate a large amount of his monthly budget to food. Our daughter is religious about packing lunch and snacks from home and budgets just five dollars per month for food. She puts the saved money into her clothing budget.

Activities

Activities include organized sports, outings with friends, clubs, and optional field trips. This is our largest budget category, and one of the hardest for us to get right over the course of the year. It's very informative for a kid to see that, of the $125 he gets every month for expenses, 40 percent (fifty dollars) gets put into the activities budget. He is better able to prioritize activities when he understands that there's a give-and-take involved with every choice: in order to take on another activity, is there something that will need to be given up? Or is there extra money in the overall budget and extra time in his schedule? These are great conversation points that will encourage the kid to assign his own priorities rather than having them dictated by the parent.

Before we began budgeting, we found the kids often wanted to participate in a different activity every day of the week. Each time a flyer came home from school, they would beg to join. Aside from the costs associated with all of the activities, we had to commit a lot of time to get the kids to and from practices and meetings.

Once we began budgeting, we could ask the kids if they had the money to pay for the latest activity. If they didn't, but we both agreed it was something they wanted to try (we recognized that, as kids, they were excited to explore new options), we brainstormed where the additional money might come from. Sometimes it meant moving money from a different category; sometimes it meant doing a few extra jobs around the house (as parents we're not above over-paying a kid for a well-done job if we know there is a specific reason they are trying to earn the money). Sometimes it came in the form of an increase in allowance if it was an activity we wanted to support.

The bottom line for our kids was that participation in every new activity wasn't a given; each had to be considered and discussed. Instead of arguments or disagreements, these were planning and prioritizing sessions. The kids were in control of their own activity schedules as long as they could make it fit within their budgets. We found this not only kept the kids from signing up for every new opportunity, but it also kept them committed to their activities once they had joined.

In our area, hockey is a very popular sport. It is also amazingly expensive. If you decide that one of these mega-sports fits your family's time and financial budget, we encourage you to put these funds into your child's budget. He (and you!) will be surprised at how large a financial commitment it is, which may lead to some conversations about personal commitment to the sport and available alternatives if he is willing to try something else. Whatever you decide, make sure your child has significant ownership in the cost. He will fully appreciate the weight his sport carries in his personal financial picture.

Clothing and Shoes

These are the next most important categories. We often find that a season has come and gone with one of these categories being exhausted, while money is left in the other. It's reasonable to allow transfers between these two categories as needed. You might consider combining these two categories into one from the very start. One advantage to keeping them separate is that it builds more discipline in budgeting and tracking and helps kids learn that budgets can be flexible—but that the cash has to come from somewhere.

Presents

It is so liberating when your child has his own funds to use for purchasing Mother's Day presents, Christmas presents, or gifts for a friend's birthday party. The thoughtfulness he will put into gift selection is refreshing. Rather than picking out something for you to buy for his friend, he's more likely to evaluate the options and spend within his budget. One of the big lessons our kids have learned from having a presents budget is that pooling resources among their three budgets allows them to buy really nice Christmas presents for Mom and Dad, rather than each of them spending ten dollars on separate (and dodgy) gifts. It's fun to watch them engage in conversation and negotiation when working together to pick out a joint gift. We've found that they're also more appreciative in general when they receive gifts; they realize that someone else has paid for it.

Charity

By saving ten dollars per month, our kids have had the opportunity to do some big things with their charity money. At first, they were eager to bring money to church every week to put in the offering plate. Now they have gotten in the habit of saving over the course of four to six months, then making a large contribution to a special campaign or an international charity, such as the organization Feed My Starving Children. Another innovative use of charity money is bidding on silent auctions; having forty dollars to bid on a basket of books or movies at a benefit dinner is not something many preteens get to do. Giving your kids the ability to make meaningful charitable contributions is a tremendous gift. Don't overlook it.

Savings

Use this category to accumulate funds for a couple of months and then take it to the bank to deposit into a savings account. Don't accumulate more than fifty dollars or so in the savings envelope or it might "disappear" in a moment of poor financial judgment. The concept of saving money is discussed in more detail in the next section, "Putting Everything into Practice."

Thinking Points

- Will these categories work for your family, or will you choose your own list of categories?
- Which categories will you start with?

Putting Everything into Practice

Just Ease into It

You should not expect your child to be immediately successful going from zero to financial genius, but there are some easy ways to scale up your plan over time. We worked with our children through the process over the course of several years, from ages nine to twelve. If you take it step by step, each stage will begin to feel easy and automatic and you will know you're ready to move on.

Start weekly and then go monthly.

Young kids are going to have trouble thinking several weeks ahead, so accommodate them by starting with a weekly allowance. If you are taking this approach, you're probably not ready to hand over large amounts of cash or to delegate spending in any important categories. A natural place to start is a weekly allowance for fun, charity, and savings.

Every Friday, hand over an allowance of three dollars for fun, one dollar for savings, and one dollar for charity. Help him realize that getting fun money every week doesn't mean it has to be spent every week. Work with him to think of things to buy that will require him to save up his fun money—this may require you to step back from always paying for everything he wants. Likewise, help him find ways to donate his charity money so that he can see the impact his money is making.

By doing all of this, you're making money management a routine. It should get predictable—boring, even. When you've reached that stage, you're ready to move on to more budget categories or longer time periods between allowance days (every two weeks or even monthly).

Handing over this level of financial responsibility is really just an extension of the Treat Sheet, without the sheet. Instead of giving your child a quarter at a time, you're giving him a few dollars at a time, every week like clockwork.

✓ Start with fewer categories.

When we used the Treat Sheet, there was really just one category: fun. The next natural step after starting a true allowance is to add more categories, like charity and savings.

For older kids, you may consider allocations into more advanced categories, but don't jump into full monthly budgeting in all categories just yet. First add a category like presents. How many presents does a ten-year-old need to buy? Usually it's limited to brothers and sisters, Mom and Dad, and maybe a classmate's birthday party. We have found that ten dollars per month works well at that age for targeting small gifts in the range of ten to twenty dollars. If you're starting an allowance with a ten-year-old, you might consider ten dollars per week, divided evenly among fun, charity, savings, and presents.

> ***Really big purchases***
>
> Using these techniques, our kids have gained skill and confidence in managing larger and larger budgets. The most recent "big win" was when the boys told us they wanted to buy their own laptop computers. We helped them out by identifying some really big jobs they could do to earn extra money. We also helped them learn how to research laptop specs on the Internet. Within six months they had saved enough, and researched enough, to make smart buys on computers costing $450-$500.
>
> It may be our imaginations, but they seem to be really careful with their new laptops. Go figure.

✓ Increase responsibility.

Once your child is used to allocating his weekly allowance into these categories, you'll want to consider moving to a monthly allowance—at first with no additional categories. Let the concept of monthly planning sink in until he's comfortable with it and then add some of the more advanced budgeting accounts. We recommend starting with shoes and/or clothing.

There is some serious budgeting involved in both the shoes and clothing categories. In Minnesota for example, we have to save money for several months each summer and fall to have the funds to buy winter boots. (Yes, a ten-year-old can be counted on to buy his own boots.) The wrong boots could blow the whole budget, so great care must be taken in deciding what footwear is purchased and when. Similarly, seasonal clothing needs dictate that there are significant purchases of summer clothes each spring, as well as back-to-school clothing purchases late in the summer. Once kids are adept at managing a budget, they are ready to manage an annual cycle of clothing purchases—it takes some skill to look forward in the year and plan purchases accordingly.

Kids will learn that it's wise to buy winter boots for next year at the end of winter (when the current year's styles are on sale), that secondhand stores have cheap (and cool!) clothes, and that if they take care of their clothes, they can *sell* them at secondhand stores when they outgrow them.

Other categories can be added when your child is ready to manage more responsibility. The final and most difficult category for a child to manage is the activities account. For many kids these days, this account will be larger than all other accounts combined. Despite the difficulty, it's key to get to this level of financial responsibility. Managing an activities budget is like the graduation test for the allowance and budgeting system—expect there to be some significant ups and downs, serious failures, and for the mastery of this category to take several years.

Thinking Points

- If you haven't already started your child on a limited allowance, what's holding you back?
- Are there spending categories you're reluctant to hand off? For example, will your children buy clothes that conform to your standards?

I Know What You're Thinking...

This is crazy!

Only exceptionally smart ten-year-olds can manage a $125 monthly budget, right?

How can I possibly teach my kid financial responsibility when I've been living paycheck to paycheck for the past ten years?

Trust us, none of this is crazy. It's a simple, stepwise progression in which you let your kids have responsibility over a portion of their financial lives. It's not going to go perfectly—it shouldn't go perfectly—because the whole point is to help your children learn some painful financial lessons while the cost of their mistakes is very small.

Your kid is going to make some bad choices, and he's going to buy some things that you think are bad ideas. Just remember:

- This is money you were going to spend on him anyway. It's not costing you anything to give your child a financial education.
- Every dollar your child spends wisely—and every financial mistake he makes—is part of the learning process. If you play your cards right, your child will have the financial sense at age sixteen that most Americans are starting to learn in their thirties and forties—if they ever learn at all.
- If you're struggling with finances, you might be surprised at the lessons and discussions you share with your child as you go through this process. The only difference between your child and you is the size of the accounts. The same basic principles apply to everyone in charge of managing a budget.

When It All Breaks Down

As we've already discussed, the system won't always work as planned. As soon as you put a new step in place and hand over more responsibility and a larger budget, it is almost certain that something will immediately break down.

Relax. This is all part of the plan.

Learning how to manage money isn't easy. You've probably already realized this yourself. The only way to learn, unfortunately, is to make a lot of mistakes. Your job as a responsible parent is to see to it that your children learn these mistakes when the consequences are minimal. In essence, you're creating opportunities for your kids to make small mistakes now so they won't have to learn with expensive mistakes later.

It might sound crazy, but you may find yourself actively encouraging your child to make a financial blunder. For example, you know that school shopping is coming up, and Junior wants to buy a pair of "cool" tennis shoes—but he also insists on buying two pairs of flip-flops for summer camp. You know that he should be saving up shoe money to buy those

> ***Stuff we tried that failed***
>
> We tried one big pile of money in each of their envelopes with registers that showed how much of that money was still left in each category. This was a mess. To learn how to manage spending, the kids needed to actually see that "shoes" was empty, but that there was still fifty dollars in "activities."
>
> When they were ten, we tried using debit cards for the kids instead of cash—another miserable failure. Our kids didn't "get" the idea of money and relative value using plastic. They needed to touch and count the bills.
>
> We tried to have both of us participate in the monthly one-on-one meetings with the kids. Tracie got way too frustrated (and upset) about some of the kids' money mistakes. Bret was able to roll with it, counsel the kids on spending more wisely, and help them move on. We learned it was best for Bret to manage those meetings solo.
>
> You're going to have issues; that's okay. Just accept them, make changes, and move on. Keep the finish line in sight.

sneakers for back-to-school and that the extra twenty dollars he spent on flip-flops is going to thwart that plan. You say nothing, however, and when back-to-school shopping comes, he realizes that he can't buy the special shoes. He has learned a lesson and now has a decision to make: buy a cheaper pair within his budget to have new shoes before school, or hold off for a couple months to buy the cool shoes he really wants?

This is a scenario that teaches very valuable life lessons—don't spoil it by warning him of what's going to happen. A child in this position is probably twelve or thirteen years old and is predisposed to resist learning anything you (or any adult) are trying to teach him. These lessons are much more vivid when Junior finds himself in a pickle—brought about by his own actions—and then has to rely on himself to plan a way out.

Letting him experience the consequence of improper planning and then the satisfaction of delayed gratification is much more important than proving to him that you were right.

When things go really wrong.

Sometimes there are serious problems. Junior is misappropriating funds from his charity account and spending it all on comic books. Or your daughter has taken eighty dollars out of clothing and spent it all on a designer fragrance. These are signs that the child is not ready to practice responsible management of his or her allowance. The solution is simple: take control of their finances for a month or two. Just take the envelopes back!

While the envelopes are in your control, you continue to fund as you previously did. Each month, you put the designated allowance into each category. When needs arise, you decide how to spend the money. You remove the money from the envelope and mark down the expense in the register. The only thing that has changed is that the child is no longer choosing how the money is spent. His envelopes still receive the same amount each month. Remember—it's **your** money in the envelope; you are just letting him manage it, **as long as he can demonstrate that he can do so responsibly.**

You will probably find that within a month or two, he will discover that he misses having control over (and access to) his money, and he will come up with a plan to avoid future financial "irregularities."

What if they don't come around?

We did this with our daughter—she "misappropriated" funds one month and went nuts on à la carte and dessert items during lunch at school (apparently spending seven dollars a day on cookies and chips isn't a problem at her school). So we took her envelope back and told her we'd manage her money while she figured out how to be responsible again.

It didn't bother her one bit. She liked having us do all of the work managing her budget. However, when we were managing the money, we got to buy the clothes. She didn't even have to be with us when we went shopping. We got to manage where the fun money went, as well—and in this case, it all went to replenish her activities fund, not to buy iTunes gift cards.

If it doesn't sink in, just start buying your child's clothes without taking her shopping with you. The "surprise" of the jeans you pick out for her might help her to snap out of her nonchalant attitude.

See where this is going? When they lose the right to responsibly manage their money, they also lose their freedom of choice, and that gets old really quick. The flip side of this example is also an important lesson.

If they're managing the money, they should have complete freedom to spend it as they choose. It's fine if your child is really into Aeropostale and not so much into Sears—as long as she can make it work within her budget, she can choose where to shop. If you're not willing to give them complete freedom, then don't delegate that budget category just yet.

Of course, you probably have standards in place for your family: ESRB ratings on video games, minimum length of skirts, and so on. If you get resistance on the limits you set, remind them that even though they're managing much of their own money, you're still paying the mortgage, the gas bill, and the medical expenses. When they're ready to take over *that* money management, they can move out and wear whatever they want.

Thinking Points

- Will you talk to your child about the potential consequences of budget problems, or let those consequences become apparent when the time arises?
- Which are the spending categories you're most worried about?
- When did you accidently overspend your budget or income? What did you learn from that mistake?

Shopping

For younger kids, shopping is an activity—it's something to do, either for the fun of it or out of boredom. Frankly, this is true for some adults, as well—but these adults tend to be either phenomenally wealthy or deep in debt.

Starting in the early teens, shopping begins to take on the aspect of a "chore"—there are times when a teen just needs to go out and buy a necessity. Most of the time, however, teens go out shopping for fun. A healthy definition of shopping is: **a fun activity to enjoy when you want to buy something and have saved the funds needed to buy it.** The word "something" is key to the definition—unhealthy shopping happens when there is not a clear idea of what's being sought. Sometimes this is an intractable problem—sometimes you don't know what you're looking for until you see it in the store. Many stores, in fact, count on this "problem" to make their sales.

We found it hard to tell our kids, "We're not going to go shopping if you can't tell us what you intend to buy."

We came up with this plan instead: "If you really want to go walk around the mall for some Sunday entertainment, and you're not planning to buy anything, that's fine. Leave your money at home and let's go window-shopping. We'll go to a couple of stores and see what's out there. At the end of the day, if you know what you need and it's in your budget, then we can make a

> ***But I just found this great deal...***
>
> It happens. You're out running errands and your daughter finds something she's been looking for—and it's on sale! But she doesn't have her money with her. How can she buy it?
>
> Remember that we're trying to avoid debt, so resist the urge to "lend her the money." You can accomplish the desired result if you buy the item yourself, save the receipt, and have her buy it from you with cash when you get home.
>
> If it turns out she doesn't have the cash, you can either return it later or secretly hang onto it for an upcoming birthday or Christmas gift!

separate trip later (or tomorrow) to buy it." This may sound like extra work—it is. We're trying to make a distinction between "shopping" and "buying," with the intent of teaching our kids how to resist the lure of impulse buying.

There is an exception to this rule: fun money. If the kid has fun money, it's perfectly fine to part with it on an impulse buy.

We encourage our kids to "window-shop" via the Sunday ads: read through everything, decide what you want or need, find where it's on sale, and verify that you have the funds to purchase it. Then we'll go over the plan, make sure the money is in the budget, and arrange for a trip to the store to buy it!

> ***A virtual shopping guru***
>
> Our children's school has a unit in seventh grade called "Family and Consumer Science" (formerly known as "Home Ec.") where students learn about shopping, saving, and budgeting. The kids were given an assignment to come up with a coordinated outfit using store ads or online shopping. They were told to stay under one hundred dollars for the complete outfit.
>
> Using coupons, checkout codes, and a lot of research, our daughter found a great outfit on the Gap website. Her total cost: seven dollars!
>
> Her teacher and classmates were amazed. Our daughter was amazed at the number of students who failed the exercise. They couldn't come up with *one* outfit for less than one hundred dollars!

There's a cool side-effect to this strategy: you're going to find that you spend a lot less time cruising the stores, either by yourself or with your kids. Our thirteen-year-old daughter knows exactly where the Kohl's discount department store is and where the clothing consignment stores are, but was surprised one day when we needed to go to our regional shopping mall to find an Apple store for computer service.

"What *is* this place?" she asked. We hadn't realized it, but our teen daughter had never been to the mall! Even without spending her weekends hanging out at the mall, she has found a way to dress in style on a budget that works for her and for us. And let's be clear: she knows the styles and how to dress. She's been known to shop for weeks for the perfect skirt to match a set of leggings and a specific sweater. She dresses well and keeps her clothing purchases within her budget. What more could we want?

Thinking Points

- How flexible will you be in lending money when the money envelope isn't brought along on a shopping trip? What will your repayment conditions be?
- Will you be willing to take your children on a shopping trip if they find something they need on sale?

Savings

We've written quite a bit about the savings category. What is "savings" and what is it used for? For how long should money be saved? How much savings is enough?

Believe it or not, your decision about how to handle savings will probably be the hardest decision that you make in helping your child develop financial discipline. One reason for this is because your idea of "the future" includes events ten or twenty years away, whereas a preteen has a hard time envisioning what life will be like after Christmas. In essence, **kids want to save money so they can spend it** (remember the Treat Sheet?), while **adults view saving money as an end in itself**.

> ***Revisiting jobs vs. chores***
>
> Way back in the "Beginnings" section, we talked about the difference between jobs and chores. We recommend that everyone in the family has chores, which represent each member pulling his own weight to make the family run.
>
> When older kids start looking for more money for a big purchase, jobs start looking really attractive: wash the windows, scrub out the garbage cans, re-organize the laundry closet. These are all jobs that adults hate to do, but a young teen will happily take them on for five dollars an hour.

Fortunately, there is a happy medium: our kids have two savings accounts. One is just a custodial checking account, while the other is what we call their "401k Kid" account. The first is for short-term savings, and the second is for the long term.

Month by month, they save money and put it into their short-term savings accounts, with a few simple rules on taking it out:

- Anything you purchase using money from savings must have prior approval.

- You can't withdraw more than half of your savings for any purchase (see the next rule).
- When you make a withdrawal from short-term savings, you will make an equal withdrawal to deposit into your 401k Kid account.

It's perfectly fine to take money from savings and use it to fund purchases, but it's also important to build up a long-term savings account to use for college, a house, or retirement. These are really "save it for later" funds that should never be taken out for short-term needs. But a kid is not capable of the discipline required to fund the long-term account. The savings transfer rule is an automatic way for them to save money for those big later-in-life purchases.

We make the pot a little sweeter by matching a portion of their deposits (similar to most 401(k) retirement accounts)—every time they make a deposit, we make a matching deposit.

How does money get into savings?

Money goes into savings in a number of ways. First, a portion of each month's allowance is put there. Next, money from gifts and jobs can be put into savings. Unexpected money from garage sales or found under the sofa cushion can be saved. Finally, any time one of our kids wants to take surplus from another category and save it instead of spending it, we give a big thumbs-up!

> ***Saving for a Vacation***
>
> Adults shouldn't be the only ones saving for a family vacation. If the kids know that you're going to Disney World next summer, they have the opportunity to save up for the trip as well.
>
> How much fun would it be as a twelve-year-old to go on vacation with one hundred dollars to spend on whatever you wanted?
>
> And how much fun would it be as a parent to not have to constantly hear from your twelve-year-old,"Daddy, can we buy this? It's only ten dollars." When they've worked for and saved their own funds, everyone has a more relaxing vacation. (And they buy a lot less junk.)

As they grow into teens, they'll start earning larger sums of money by working jobs—babysitting, mowing lawns, and walking dogs can all lead to big paydays, even for young teens. We have established this guideline for earned money:

Every time you get paid, ten dollars goes into your fun account, and the rest goes into savings.

When our daughter was twelve, she worked as a mother's helper two days a week during the summer. The neighbor, a work-at-home mother, was so happy with her newfound productivity that she was paying our daughter twenty dollars twice a week. Each time she earned money, ten dollars went into the fun envelope, and ten dollars went into savings. Using this system, she had an additional twenty dollars in spending money every week, and she was putting twenty dollars into savings as well. By the end of the summer, she had managed to put nearly three hundred dollars into savings from this and other jobs. This was the same girl who couldn't save $160 for a plane ticket just three years prior.

When should kids withdraw from savings?

A recurring theme in this book is that the kids are in charge of their own spending. You can believe that if there's money in their savings accounts, they have a few ideas on how to spend it. They are really performing the Treat Sheet trick, but with a much larger account. When they've saved up enough to purchase their goal items, they will let you know.

We also encourage you to have regular discussions about upcoming trips, activities, or big purchases. If you know what they're saving for, you will be more prepared for and engaged in their purchases. And when they know about big family events or upcoming activities, they may wish to change their savings plan to match. Remember, kids are visual—don't be afraid to have them continue making their own versions of charts and Treat Sheets as they grow.

Thinking Points

- How can you encourage your kid to take on extra work to put more money into savings?
- How do you feel about challenging your kid to always have something he wants set up as a savings goal?

The 401k Kid Account

Just as you (should) have a retirement savings account that is never touched for any reason, your kid should have a long-term savings account, as well. This is where money goes to buy a car at age seventeen, to pay for college expenses, or to furnish his first apartment. Money starts going into this account when he's five, and doesn't start coming out until he's making long-term "adult" decisions.

In our house, we call it the 401k Kid Account because, like most employee accounts, we offer a match on deposits. Whenever they put money into this account, we match it dollar-for-dollar. This may or may not work for you, depending on your family's financial position, but we encourage you to give it a try, at least in the beginning when the contributions are probably going to be pretty small. You will be surprised at how this account grows over the years, and also at the sense of pride (and appreciation) your child has for the money it contains. You both know how hard he's worked to fund it, and you also know that by the time he's old enough to spend it, he will have learned the lessons needed to be able to spend it wisely.

We are still years away from taking money out of the 401k Kid Accounts in our family, but we have a number of rules and expectations we have laid out for our kids—the most important of which is: **no withdrawals before age sixteen.** We're figuring out the rest as we go, including ways to invest these funds. We are helping the kids learn some lessons in investing with their 401k Kid Accounts before they are thrust into real money lessons with future 401(k) accounts.

Stay tuned for our next book, in which we follow our kids into their teens, sharing the lessons they learn as they use more advanced budgeting techniques and learn to independently manage their 401k Kid Accounts.

Conclusion

Your kids need a solid financial education now to avoid costly financial mistakes later. It doesn't matter how young they are—or how old. This is a process that you should start **today** to achieve the best results.

- Ages four and under: start with understanding the value of money.
- Ages four to six: use the Treat Sheet to encourage saving toward a goal.
- Ages six to nine: use a small allowance, weekly at first, to manage charity, savings, and fun, to teach the basics of budgeting.
- Ages nine and up: work toward a larger allowance, eventually given monthly, that covers all of the child's annual expenses.

Whatever age your child is, there's a place to start. Each older age group should be able to quickly master the earlier concepts. Using the approach we have outlined, you will end up with a sixteen-year-old who is capable of calculating what her annual and monthly allowance should be in each of her spending categories, and who can effectively manage and track spending each month while staying within her budget.

There will be many mistakes made along the way, and some of them will be painful. This is part of the plan! These painful mistakes made early-on can prevent a nineteen-year-old (or a twenty-nine-year-old!) from getting into serious financial trouble. If you're like us, you know how painful these adult financial mistakes are, and how long it can take to recover from them. We only wish that we had learned these lessons in our teens rather than in our thirties.

The core message of this book is this: **financial responsibility is only gained after making painful personal financial mistakes.**

A sixteen-year-old can't make financial mistakes if you're always telling her exactly what she can or cannot do with her money. If you want your child to learn financial responsibility, then get comfortable giving her enough money and responsibility to be dangerous—then get out of her way!

We have been working for the last ten years to give our kids an understanding of the value of money and the discipline needed to manage a monthly budget. They are now each managing over $160 per month, which is starting to feel like a lot of money—both for them and for us.

We sincerely hope each of them makes one really boneheaded, heartbreaking money mistake this year.

They'll thank us later.

Made in the USA
Monee, IL
04 November 2026

67380523R00039